# IT'S TIME TO EAT BEAN SALAD

# It's Time to Eat
# BEAN SALAD

## Walter the Educator

Silent King Books
A WhichHead Entertainment Imprint

Copyright © 2024 by Walter the Educator

All rights reserved. No part of this book may be reproduced in any manner whatsoever without written per- mission except in the case of brief quotations embodied in critical articles and reviews.

First Printing, 2024

## Disclaimer

This book is a literary work; the story is not about specific persons, locations, situations, and/or circumstances unless mentioned in a historical context. Any resemblance to real persons, locations, situations, and/or circumstances is coincidental. This book is for entertainment and informational purposes only. The author and publisher offer this information without warranties expressed or implied. No matter the grounds, neither the author nor the publisher will be accountable for any losses, injuries, or other damages caused by the reader's use of this book. The use of this book acknowledges an understanding and acceptance of this disclaimer.

It's Time to Eat BEAN SALAD is a collectible early learning book by Walter the Educator suitable for all ages belonging to Walter the Educator's Time to Eat Book Series. Collect more books at WaltertheEducator.com

**USE THE EXTRA SPACE TO TAKE NOTES AND DOCUMENT YOUR MEMORIES**

# BEAN SALAD

It's time to eat, come take a seat,

# It's Time to Eat

# Bean Salad

A bowl of beans that's hard to beat!

Colors and shapes, both big and small,

Bean salad's here to please us all!

Black beans shiny, soft, and round,

Pinto beans with a speckled sound.

Kidney beans so red and sweet,

Together they're a tasty treat!

Green beans crunchy, snap and chew,

Chickpeas golden, just for you.

Lima beans so smooth and light,

Bean salad makes your day so bright!

Tomatoes chopped with peppers too,

Add some onions, just a few.

Drizzle on dressing, give it a mix,

A yummy snack that's quick to fix!

# It's Time to Eat

# Bean Salad

Spoonfuls of flavor, bite by bite,

Healthy and fresh, it feels just right.

Beans are magic, strong and neat,

A perfect food for us to eat!

Protein power in every bean,

They keep us strong and feeling keen.

A little bowl, or maybe more,

Bean salad's something to adore!

Share it with friends, pass it around,

Laughter and smiles will surely abound.

Eating together is always so fun,

Bean salad joy for everyone!

Morning, lunch, or dinner time,

Bean salad fits, it's just sublime.

A tasty dish, so full of cheer,

# It's Time to Eat

# Bean Salad

Let's dig in, our meal is here!

One last bite, then we all say,

"Thank you, beans, for a great day!"

Nature's gift, so fresh and true,

Bean salad is the best for you!

So grab your fork, and don't delay,

Bean salad makes a brighter day.

Eat it up, feel strong and bright,

## It's Time to Eat

# Bean Salad

Beans are fuel, pure delight!

# ABOUT THE CREATOR

Walter the Educator is one of the pseudonyms for Walter Anderson. Formally educated in Chemistry, Business, and Education, he is an educator, an author, a diverse entrepreneur, and he is the son of a disabled war veteran. "Walter the Educator" shares his time between educating and creating. He holds interests and owns several creative projects that entertain, enlighten, enhance, and educate, hoping to inspire and motivate you. Follow, find new works, and stay up to date with Walter the Educator™ at WaltertheEducator.com

www.ingramcontent.com/pod-product-compliance
Lightning Source LLC
LaVergne TN
LVHW052010060526
838201LV00059B/3958